THE DAYS OF CREATION

Simon Turpin

DayOne

*"To my wife Jessica, thank you
for all your love and support."*

The days of Creation
Simon Turpin

ISBN 978-1-84625-571-7

Cover design and typesetting by Dave Hewer Design (davehewer.com)
Printed by Orchard Press Cheltenham Ltd

British Library Cataloguing in Publication Data available.

Contents

Did God really say six days?

For most people in the Church today the length of the Days of Creation in Genesis 1 is generally seen as unimportant. This is largely due to the influence of Darwinian evolution and the idea that the world is millions of years old. Many Christians now reject Genesis 1 as a historical account of the creation of the world in six 24-hour days. Some believe the days to be long periods of time (progressive creationists), in which the long ages of evolutionary history took place. And others, who understand the account to be poetic (theistic evolutionists), argue that Genesis is not about when or how God created the world.

These interpretations, sadly, have nothing to do with what the Bible clearly teaches but come from outside ideas being imposed upon it. As Christians, we need to realise that God's Word has been under attack ever since the Garden of Eden when the serpent asked *"did God actually say?"*(Genesis 3:1). In fact, the apostle Paul issued a warning to the Corinthian Church:

But I am afraid that as the serpent deceived Eve by his cunning, your thoughts will be led astray from a sincere and pure devotion to Christ. (2 Corinthians 11:3).

Satan's method of deception with Eve was to get her to question God's Word. Unfortunately, many of God's people have fallen for this deception and are questioning the authority of God's Word when it comes to Genesis 1-11. We must understand that in our era of history, especially since the 18th Century, the attack on God's word has been mainly upon the historicity of Genesis 1-11.

But why all the fuss concerning one word: 'day', especially one that appears to have such little impact on Christian theology? Is it because the Bible is not clear enough? Actually, the Bible is really clear about how long God took to create, consider what God said to His people in the fourth commandment:

For in six days the LORD made heaven and earth, the sea, and all that is in them, and rested on the seventh day. Exodus 20:11

In fact, this is how most scholars understood Genesis 1 before the 18th Century, including the first century Jewish historian Josephus[1], the early church fathers Lactantius and Basil the Bishop of Caesarea, as well as the Reformers Martin Luther[2] and John Calvin.

As Christians, we need to recognise that belief in the world being supernaturally created by God, in six 24-hour days, is important for a coherent, logical, and internally consistent understanding of the biblical message of creation, fall, and redemption (Romans 5:12–21; 8:19-22; Acts

"Genesis 1-11 is the foundation to the rest of the Bible and if we remove it then the rest of the Bible will collapse around it."

17:22–34). Think about it, if you remove the foundation to a house then what will happen to it? It will collapse! We must realise that all our doctrine, either directly or indirectly, is founded upon the historicity of Genesis 1-11: sin, death, seven-day week, marriage, restoration of creation etc. Genesis 1-11 is the foundation to the rest of the Bible and if we remove it then the rest of the Bible will collapse around it.

A verse to remember

A verse to remember: Every word of God proves true... Do not add to his words, lest he rebuke you and you be found a liar. Proverbs 30:5-6

The question we need to ask now is: what does Genesis 1 tell us about the length of days and what the original creation was like? It is important to understand that the idea of the great age of the earth came from the belief that the fossil record was laid down over millions of years. The fossil record contains the record of the deaths of billions of creatures. In fact, it is a horrible record of death, disease, suffering and cruelty. Therefore, the interpretation of Genesis 1 is crucial in understanding discussions about evolution and the age of the earth.

For example, if Genesis 1 teaches that creation took place in six 24-hour days, which indicates a young earth, then it rules out the millions of years

"...the idea of the great age of the earth came from the belief that the fossil record was laid down over millions of years."

claimed as fact by secular scientists for the age of the earth.

There are a number of reasons Genesis 1 rules out any long age evolutionary ideas that are often imposed upon it.

First, the key point in understanding the length of the days in Genesis 1 is that they are in fact numbered and are used with the qualifiers "evening" and "morning". God, therefore, defines the days by those contextual clues, for example day one: "And there was evening and there was morning, the first day." Furthermore, Exodus 20:8–11 gives a clear indication that the days are 24 hours long.

Second, the Bible tells us that God's word brought creation into existence (Psalm 33:6, 9). In Genesis 1, the divine command "let there be" is followed by "and there was" which reveals rapid fulfilment of that command with no process:

- ▷ Narration: "God said…"
- ▷ Commandment: "let there be…"
- ▷ Fulfilment: "and there was"
- ▷ Evaluation: "God saw that it was good"
- ▷ And conclusion: "there was evening and morning"

This structure is used in the first six days of creation (Day 7 is not a day of creation but a day of rest: see Genesis 2:1–3) and shows that God's powerful creative activity occurred within those six days.

Third, in Genesis 1:26–27, God made the first man and woman in His own image and distinct from the animals. From a biblical perspective, mankind is not just a random accident or a glorified ape, but is the crowning glory of God's creation (Psalm 8:3–9).

Fourth, Genesis 1:29–30 indicates that man and animals had a vegetarian diet before the Fall, which, of course, rules out any carnivorous activity. Although some argue that the eating of plants would involve their death, this overlooks the fact that plants are not described in the Bible as "living creatures" as man and the animals are. The words used to describe their termination are more descriptive such as "wither" or "fade" (Psalm 37:2, 102:11; Isaiah 64:6). Even after the Fall, Adam and Eve were to eat the herb of the field (Genesis 3:17–19), and it was not until after the Flood that man could eat meat (Genesis 9:3). The Fall in Genesis 3 would best explain the origin of carnivorous animal behaviour.

Fifth, God had already stated six times that His creation was "good" (vv. 4, 10, 12, 18, 21, 25). However, at the end of Day Six God saw all that He had made and declared it to be "very good" (v. 31). When "good" is modified by "very", it is implying much more than a beautiful creation. The phrase "very good" indicates that God created the world perfect with no death or suffering in it.

From an understanding of the genealogies in Genesis 5 and 11,[3] this seven-day week would have occurred around 6,000 years ago, thus ruling out any interpretation that tries to accommodate the current evolutionary framework of cosmology, geology, and anthropology with the Scripture.[4] Therefore, the time frame that the Bible gives for God creating the world, rules out any old-earth or evolutionary interpretation of Genesis 1.

A verse to remember:

For in six days the LORD made heaven and earth, the sea, and all that is in them, and rested on the seventh day.

Exodus 20:11

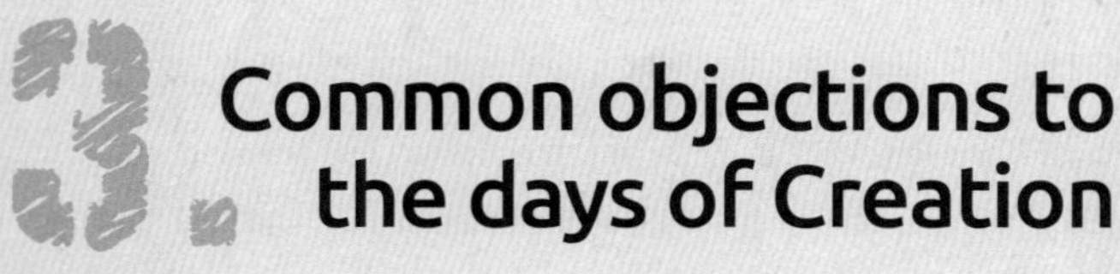

Common objections to the days of Creation

There are number of common objections given by Christians as to why the days of creation are not 24 hours. Nevertheless, under closer examination these objections fail.

Gap theory

The "gap theory" is the belief that there is a gap of indeterminate time between in Genesis 1:1 and Genesis 1:2. The grammar of Genesis 1, however, does not allow for this. Genesis 1:2 is an explanation of what the earth was like when God first created it.[5] The account of events begins in Genesis 1:1 and continues through to Genesis 1:3. Verse 2 is not part of the sequence of events but is a parenthetical statement describing the original condition of the earth. In Genesis 1:2 the earth is without form and void but Genesis 1:3–31 will tell of how God formed and filled up His creation. Moreover, Exodus 20:11 states that God made everything in six days. And the verse says He made the earth during those six days. So this is further evidence that Day One begins in Genesis 1:1 and ends in 1:5.

The Sun was not created until day four

One of the main objections to interpreting the days of Genesis 1 as 24-hour days is that since the sun is not created until Day Four, the first three days cannot be ordinary days. However, this is not a problem with the text but is based on the presupposition that the sun is necessary to have a day marked by evening and morning. But to have an evening and morning on the first three days, all that is needed is a light source, which God created on Day One (Genesis 1:3), and a rotating earth. These should not be called "solar days" as the word "solar" means "related to the sun." But they were 24-hour days. The Bible tells us that God created light on Day One (Genesis 1:3), yet it does not tell us what the source was. God is not dependent upon the sun to produce the phenomenon of light. Paul, for example, was blinded by a source other than the sun on the road to Damascus (Acts 9:3). The Bible also states that God is light (1 John 1:5).

Genesis 2:4

Genesis 2:4 states: "These are the generations of the heavens and the earth when they were created, in the day that the LORD God made the earth and the heavens." It is argued that this is an example of the word "day" not meaning an ordinary day. However, the word "day" here is not qualified by a number or used with qualifiers "evening and "morning". In Genesis 2:4 the clause "in the day" is referring to a general period of time. This does not suggest that the days in Genesis 1 are non-literal days. The contextual clues in Genesis 2:4 surrounding "in the day" (i.e., "in the day that the LORD made heaven and earth") serve to indicate that a general time period is in view (i.e., the whole Creation Week of six literal days).

A verse to remember

Now these Jews were more noble than those in Thessalonica; they received the word with all eagerness, examining the Scriptures daily to see if these things were so. Acts 17:11

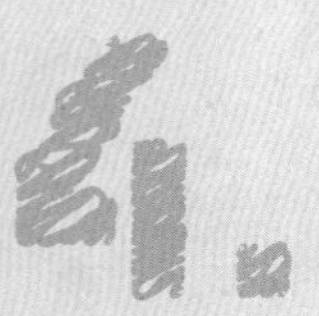

Why don't you believe in science?

Have you ever heard one of these claims by non-Christians?

"Science proves the Bible is wrong."

"Evolution is science, but the Bible is religion."

"Evolutionists believe in science, but creationists reject science."

The confusion here often lies in how people define science. People are generally unaware that dictionaries give a root meaning of science similar to this one from Oxford dictionary: "denoting knowledge." Although there are other uses of the word, the root meaning of science is basically "knowledge."

To help people understand the issue it is helpful to distinguish between two types of modern science: observational and historical science.

For instance, historical science has to do with

one's beliefs about distinct, non-observable events that happened in the past. On the other hand, observational science encompasses finding out about how things in the present world operate and being able to repeat, observe, and test those findings. When it comes to the debate over creation and evolution, we must understand that Darwinian evolution is part of historical science and not observational science. There is no empirical evidence whatsoever for Darwinian evolution (i.e., the belief that natural processes could explain the evolution of life as we see it from simple beginnings). Creationists do not deny natural selection or mutations, but they do deny that these processes produce the necessary changes that would increase genetic information and change one kind of creature into a different kind (e.g., a fish into an amphibian or a reptile into a mammal or bird). Evolutionists have failed to observe even one example of this. The evolutionary story of planet earth is not based on observational evidence but is part of their secular faith which denies supernatural revelation.

It is also important to understand that modern science came about through the working out of a particular worldview (your belief about the world), and that worldview was Christianity. For example, you need to believe there is law

and order in the world before you go out there looking for it. In fact, the universe needs to be orderly in order for science to work. But why should the universe be orderly if it is just a cosmic accident? The universe obeys certain laws and is orderly because God is a lawgiver and a God of order. In fact, most of the founders of the branches of modern science were Christians: Physics: Isaac Newton, Michael Faraday, James Clark Maxwell; Chemistry: John Dalton, Robert Boyle; Biology: Gregor Mendel, Louis Pasteur; Geology: Nicolas Steno, Adam

Sedgwick; Astronomy: Nicolaus Copernicus, Johannes Kepler.

It is important to remember that science is interpreted through a worldview. For example, what does this say?

GODISNOWHERE

If you are an atheist, because of your worldview, you would probably say: GOD IS NO WHERE but if you are a Christian, because of your worldview, you would say: GOD IS NOW HERE. This is not a matter of the evidence, but about how you interpret the evidence.

The debate over creation and evolution is not a battle between science and the Bible but between two different worldviews—naturalism and biblical theism—and how the observed physical evidence (e.g., rock layers, fossils, redshift of starlight, DNA or anatomical similarities) is to be interpreted in light of them. Rejecting evolution and the idea of millions of years is not rejecting science but rejecting a belief system.

A verse to remember

For his invisible attributes, namely, his eternal power and divine nature, have been clearly perceived, ever since the creation of the world, in the things that have been made. So they are without excuse. Romans 1:20

The Big Bang

Astronomy is one of those scientific fields that is often used to challenge the Bible. For example, you may have heard people say that the days in Genesis 1 cannot be 24 hours because of the big bang or distant star light. Nevertheless, when we really understand the cosmos, there are, as we would expect, a number of ways it affirms biblical creation and declares the glory of God (Psalm 19:1).

In contrast to the Bible, many scientists believe that the universe came into existence 13.8 billion years ago in an event called the big bang. It is important to point out to people that the big bang is a belief about the origin of the universe based upon philosophical naturalism (the belief that nature is all there is and that everything, including origins, can be explained by time, chance, and the laws of nature) used to interpret the observational data.

The big bang contradicts the biblical account of creation in several ways. First, accepting the big bang model is to ignore what the Creator has revealed

concerning how He created the universe. The Bible clearly teaches that God created everything in heaven and earth supernaturally by His word within six days (Exodus 20:11; 31:17). Second, in the big bang theory, many stars existed for billions of years before the earth, but the Bible teaches that the stars were made (rather than "appeared," as the dry land did in Genesis 1:9) three days after the earth. Finally, the Bible also teaches that the earth was completely covered with water (Genesis 1:2–9;2 Peter 3:5); whereas the evolutionary model teaches that the earth started out as molten rock and has never been completely covered with water.

The Bible is right concerning the age of the cosmos. There are many lines of observational scientific evidence that confirm the universe is only thousands of years old. One of these is the excess internal heat of three of the four giant planets. Jupiter emits twice as much energy as it receives from the sun, but such a process could not last billions of years. For example, when you take a baked potato out of the microwave, that heat is radiated out into the atmosphere. However, the heat will not radiate out forever since it only has so much heat to give out. Eventually, it will cool off. Jupiter (the size of about ten earths across) is not going to cool off very much in a few thousand years, but if it were billions of years old, then why is it not an icicle by now? This is a problem for the secular view of the cosmos. Other things like the decay of the earth's magnetic field, the recession of the moon from the earth and the existence of comets also point to a young universe (for more information visit www. answersingenesis.org).

A verse to remember

The heavens declare the glory of God, and the sky above proclaims his handiwork. Psalm 19:1

Death came through one man

Death and disease are a heartbreaking reality of the world we live in and daily we hear news stories of people dying as a result of natural disasters, terrorist attacks, disease and crime. People often ask why death exists in the world if there is a loving God and many simply assume that death is a natural part of life.

This is because Charles Darwin's book The Origin of Species has impacted the interpretation of Genesis 1–3 more than anything else. In his book he wrote what was essentially a history of death and suffering. He described the modern world as having arisen from "the war of nature, from famine and death", understanding death to have always been a permanent part of the world.

The Bible, on the other hand, teaches that human physical and spiritual death, together with the death of animals, came about through the disobedience of Adam (Genesis 1:29-31; 2:17; 3:8, 17-19; Romans 5:12–21; 8:19–22; 1 Corinthians 15:22–55; Colossians 1:15–21; Revelation 21:4; 22:3).

Yet, if we reject that physical death came about because of Adam's disobedience then there really is no need for the Cross, atonement, or a new heaven and earth. Biblically, all of these are needed because death and suffering entered into the creation through Adam's disobedience toward God in Genesis 3.

The Bible also describes death as an "enemy" (1 Corinthians 15:26) which implies that it is not natural and therefore cannot have been part of the original state of creation in which God created humanity. In Romans 5:14 Paul says death reigned from the time of Adam, while Romans 5:21 suggests that the dominion of death is tied to that of sin since "sin reigned in death." It was Adam's disobedience (Genesis 2:17, 3:6–19) that brought death into the world, which is why Paul believes death to be an enemy that needs to be destroyed.

Jesus' Resurrection was ultimately a victory over

death, which is why we even see our Lord outraged over the physical death of his friend Lazarus (John 11:35). We are told in John 11:33 that Jesus was "deeply moved" and the verb in Greek (embrimaomai) speaks of deep seated anger not just mere emotional upheaval. Why was Jesus angry? Because of the power of sin and death that was reigning in the world. Jesus came to overcome death and we need to live in the light of that fact.

It was through Adam that death entered into the world and it was through Christ, the Last Adam, that death was conquered.

A verse to remember

For as in Adam all die, so also in Christ shall all be made alive. 1 Corinthians 15:22

The Flood: Key to the age of the earth

When many people think about the flood in Noah's day they see it as a bedtime story or a myth. For children's books have an image of Noah's Ark that is often small and cramped with giraffe heads sticking out of the top. However, we must realize that the Bible presents the flood as a real historical event and the Ark as a massive sea worthy vessel (it would have been around 510 feet long and 51 feet tall).

Before, we look at the global flood it is important to think about a question that is often asked, regarding God's purpose for the flood: "If God is good, how could He be so capricious as to wipe out all those innocent people in the Flood?" This is not an uncommon objection raised by people who do not believe in the God of the Bible. However, this objection does not take time to consider the biblical context of the Flood. The judgement at the time of the Flood was not a result of God's supposed capriciousness; rather He had several reasons for His judgement:

> The wickedness of man.
> Every intent of the thoughts of man's heart was only evil continually.
> The earth was corrupt.
> The earth was filled with violence.
> All flesh had corrupted their way upon the earth. (Genesis 6:5,11-12)

Despite man's wickedness, God showed Himself to be gracious in that He patiently waited, presumably for people to repent, while the Ark was being prepared.

The global Flood is key to understanding the age

of the earth. The idea of the great age of the earth came from the belief that the fossil record was laid down over millions of years. However, either the fossil record is the evidence of millions of years, or it is largely the evidence of Noah's Flood. It cannot be both. We cannot logically believe in millions of years and a global Flood.

For this reason, many old-earth creationists and theistic evolutionists believe that the Flood mentioned in Genesis 6–9 was either a local flood or a myth. However, the Genesis account of the Flood is clearly a historic global catastrophe in which only Noah and his family were saved (1 Peter 3:20). This is asserted by the text itself (Genesis 6:13, 17; 7:11–12; 7:17–24) and by Jesus and the Apostles (Luke 17:26–27; 2 Peter 3:5–6).

Two major problems for rejecting the Flood as a historical global catastrophe are: (1) after the Flood God made a covenant never to destroy the earth again by a flood. However, if the Flood were only local then God has broken this promise as there have been many local floods since then. (2) Jesus speaks of the Flood of Noah as an analogy of the judgment to come at the end of the age (Matthew 24:37–39), so if the judgment in Noah's day was local then so must be the one at the end of age.

A verse to remember

I establish my covenant with you, that never again shall all flesh be cut off by the waters of the flood, and never again shall there be a flood to destroy the earth. Genesis 9:11

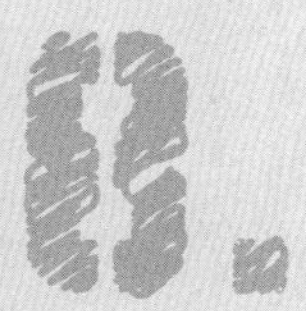

Jesus our Creator

For Christians, Jesus is more than a good teacher, a prophet or even a created being. He is in actual fact the Creator of all things, who existed before the creation of the world (John 17:5). Genesis 1:1 tells us that "In the beginning God created the heavens and the earth." In John 1:1 we read the same words, "In the beginning…" John informs us in John 1:1 that in the beginning was the Word and that the Word was not only with God but was God. This Word is the one who brought all things into being at creation (John 1:3). Several verses later, John writes that the Word who was with God in the beginning "became flesh and dwelt among us" (John 1:14).

John uses a very particular term here, "dwelt," which means he "tabernacled" among us. This is a direct parallel to the Old Testament record of when God "dwelt" in the tabernacle that Moses told the Israelites to construct (Exodus 25:8–9, 33:7). John is telling us that God "dwelt" in the physical body of Jesus.

Scripture clearly tells us that Jesus created the world by the spoken word (Hebrews 11:3) and it also reveals how this took place: "For He spoke, and it was done; He commanded, and it stood fast" (Psalm 33:9). The New Testament bears witness to this through the miracles of Jesus in the Gospels. His first (sign) miracle revealed His glory as the Creator, when He turned water into wine (John 2:1–11). We see the instant nature of His miracles very clearly in His encounter with the Roman centurion in Matthew 8:5–13 where the centurion's servant was healed the very moment Jesus commanded it. In fact, all His miracles were instantaneous (e.g., Mark 10:52; Luke 18:42–43). So when Jesus, the Word, spoke the divine command "Let there be light" (Genesis 1:3), we have very good reasons to conclude that it did not take millions of years for it to come into existence.

Furthermore, since Jesus is the one who created the world

and everything in it, He has something to say when it comes to science, history and philosophy. The reason Paul emphasises the centrality of Jesus in the life of the Church is that he wants them to know it is in Him that "are hidden all the treasures of wisdom and knowledge" (Colossians 2:3). For Christians, this is a statement relevant to all other philosophical statements regarding origins. Paul is saying that all knowledge, not just spiritual knowledge, is to be found in Jesus. Therefore, Jesus triumphs over all other claims of wisdom and knowledge because of the fact that He is the Creator of all things and therefore knows all things.

A verse to remember

In the beginning was the Word, and the Word was with God, and the Word was God. John 1:1

What did Jesus believe about Genesis?

Firstly, it is important to note that Jesus had the highest view of Scripture. Jesus clearly believed that Scripture was God's Word and therefore truth (John 17:17) and that it could not "be broken" (John 10:35). His own view of the Scripture was that each word was given by God (Matthew 4:4). For Jesus, Scripture is not merely inspired in its general ideas or its broad claims or in its general meaning, but is inspired down to its very words (Matthew 5:18).

> *"Jesus regarded the Old Testament's historicity as perfect, accurate and reliable."*

Jesus regarded the Old Testament's historicity as perfect, accurate and reliable. He often chose for illustrations in His teaching the very persons and events that are the least acceptable to people today. This can be seen from his reference to Adam (Matthew 19:4–5), Abel (Matthew 23:35), Noah (Matthew 24:37–39), Abraham (John 8:39–41, 56–58), Lot and Sodom and Gomorrah (Luke 17:28–32).

Moreover, there are multiple passages in the New Testament where Jesus quotes from the early chapters of Genesis in a straightforward, historical manner.

Matthew 19:4–6 is especially significant as Jesus quotes from both Genesis 1:27 and Genesis 2:24. Jesus' use of Scripture here is authoritative in settling a dispute over the question of divorce, as it is grounded in the creation of the first marriage and the purpose thereof (Malachi 2:14–15). The passage is also striking in understanding Jesus' use of Scripture as He attributes the words spoken as coming from the Creator (Matthew 19:4). More importantly, there is no indication in the passage that He understood it figuratively or as an allegory. If Christ were mistaken about the account of creation and its importance to marriage, then why should He be trusted when it comes to other aspects of His teaching? Furthermore,

in a parallel passage in Mark 10:6 Jesus said, "But from the beginning of creation, God 'made them male and female.'" In the statement "from the beginning of creation" Jesus was saying that Adam and Eve were there at the beginning of creation, on Day Six, not billions of years after the beginning.

From Jesus' understanding of Genesis 1–2 it is clear that He believed in the account of creation and therefore the supernatural creation of Adam as the first man and He leaves no room for the evolutionary timeline of the origin of man. Jesus clearly understood that Abel lived at the foundation of the world. This means that as the parents of Abel, Adam and Eve must also have been historical.

It is clear that Jesus accepted the book of Genesis as historical and reliable. Jesus also made a strong connection between Moses' teaching and his own

(John 5:45–47), and Moses made some very astounding claims about six-day creation in the Ten Commandments, which he says were penned by God's own hand (Exodus 20:11; 31:17-18).

People say they do not accept the Bible's account of origins in Genesis when it speaks of God creating supernaturally in six consecutive days and destroying the world in a global catastrophic flood. This cannot be said, however, without overlooking the clear teaching of our Creator, the Lord Jesus, on the matter (Mark 10:6; cf. Matthew 24:37–39) and the clear testimony of Scripture (Genesis 1:1–2, 3:6–9; Exodus 20:11; 2 Peter 3:3–6), which He affirmed as truth (Matthew 5:17–18; John 10:25, 17:17). If we confess Jesus is our Lord, we must be willing to submit to Him as the teacher of the Church.

A verse to remember

But from the beginning of creation, 'God made them male and female.' Mark 10:6

Sola Scriptura: Scripture Alone

On October 31, 1517, a German monk named Martin Luther nailed 95 theses to the door of the Castle Church in Wittenberg. This is generally considered to be the beginning of the Protestant Reformation. By posting the theses, Luther was not only condemning the Roman Catholic Church for selling indulgences (supposedly for the forgiveness of sins and release from purgatory), but he was also calling for an examination of what the Scriptures taught about indulgences.

Luther was convinced that the Bible alone was the final authority of what we should believe. Today, the Bible's authority has been reduced to areas of faith and practice. However, it is misleading to limit Scripture's authority only to these matters. Biblical doctrine is linked to history and science; therefore, whatever Scripture affirms on these matters is true. For example, the doctrine of the Resurrection understands that Jesus rose from the dead on the third day. However, naturalistic scientists would say that it is impossible for dead men to rise. Jesus also taught a recent creation and believed in the historical account of the global Flood in Noah's day, but again, naturalistic scientists would not believe such things.

Sola Scriptura has always been an issue for the people of God. In the Garden of Eden, God told Adam that if he ate from the tree of the knowledge of good and evil he would "surely die" (Genesis 2:17). Yet the Serpent told Eve, "You will not surely die" (3:4). How should they have decided the truth on this matter? Majority vote, subjective opinion, or some other way? No, they should have listened to the voice of their Creator. Instead, Eve was deceived by Satan to believe that God's Word was not sufficient; rather than believing His Word as the standard for determining truth, she decided to take matters into her own hands (verse 6). There are only tragic consequences for rejecting God's Word as our standard for life.

Because of the Church's acceptance of evolution and

millions of years, a new reformation is needed to call the Church back to trust in God's Word where it is most under attack: the history of Genesis 1–11. Much of the Bible's teaching on Creation, the Fall, Sin, Salvation, and Redemption has been eroded by the acid of evolution and millions of years.

At the time of the Protestant Reformation, the Church returned to the teaching of the Word of God and turned the world upside down. We once again need to see the church transformed by returning to the Scriptures. The church today needs to return to the principle of Sola Scriptura and to boldly preach and teach the Biblical account of creation and redemption set forth in Scripture.

A verse to remember

All Scripture is breathed out by God and profitable for teaching, for reproof, for correction, and for training in righteousness. 2 Timothy 3:16

Endnotes

1 Flavius Josephus, *The Works of Flavius Josephus*, trans. W. Whiston (London, United Kingdom: Ward, Lock & Bowden, 1987), 1.1.1; 1.3.2

2 Martin Luther, *Luther's Works Volume 1: Lectures on Genesis, Chapters 1–5*, ed. J. J. Pelikan (St. Louis, MO: Concordia Publishing House, 1958), 3–5

3 For a persuasive analysis and defence of a no-gap chronology in Genesis 5–11, see Travis R. Freeman, "Do the Genesis 5 and 11 Genealogies Contain Gaps?" in Mortenson and Ury, eds., *Coming To Grips with Genesis*, 283–313.

4 The current scientific paradigm of the origin of the universe is in the realm of historical science and not observational science.

5 See Mathews for a defence of this traditional understanding of Genesis 1:1–2. Mathews, *Genesis 1–11:26*, 136–144.

What does the Bible really say about...?
Eating Disorders
Emma Scrivener
What does the Bible really say about...?

Discussion questions
available to download online.

youth.dayone.co.uk

What does the Bible
really say about...?